French Bulldogs

Faith Woodland

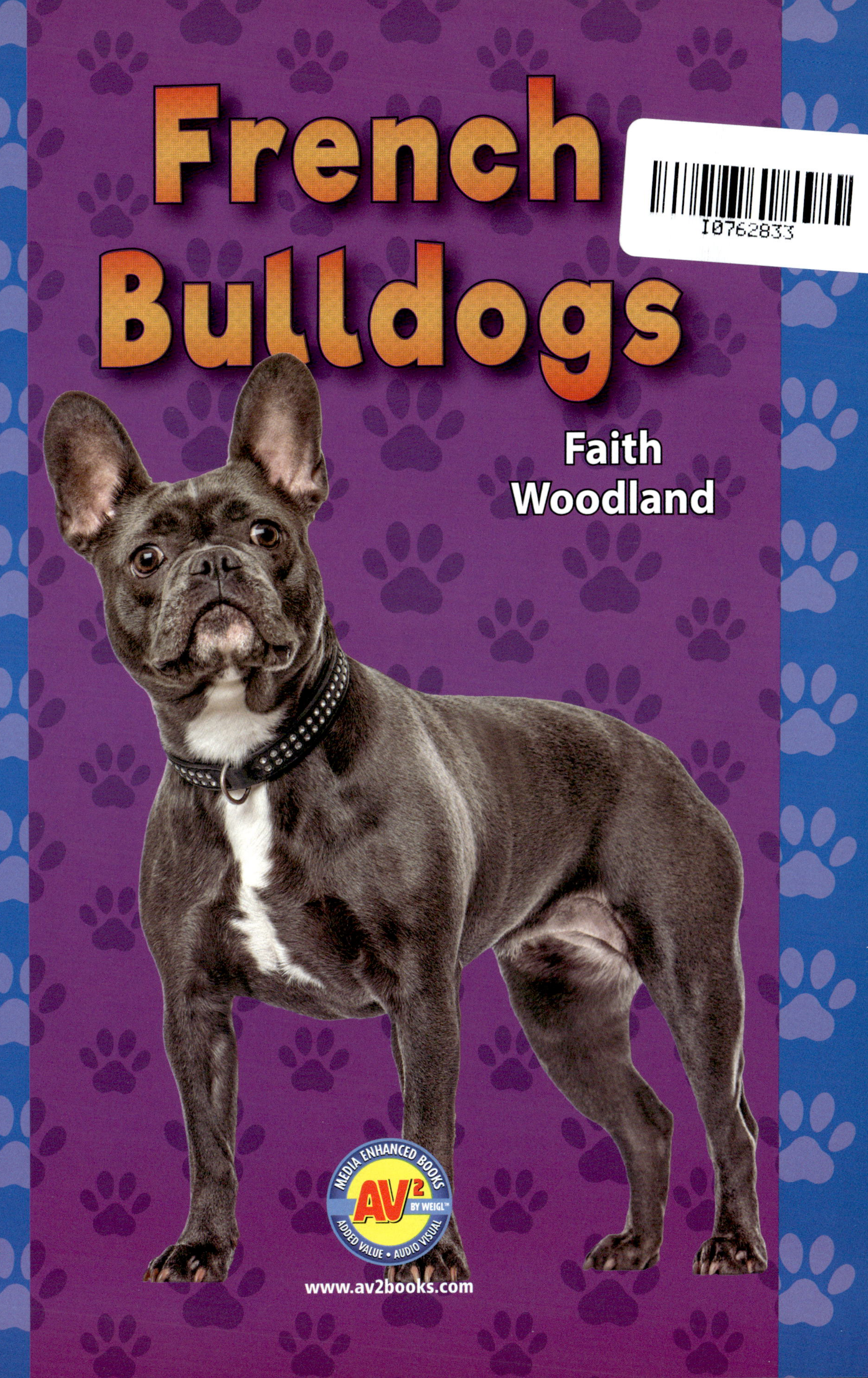

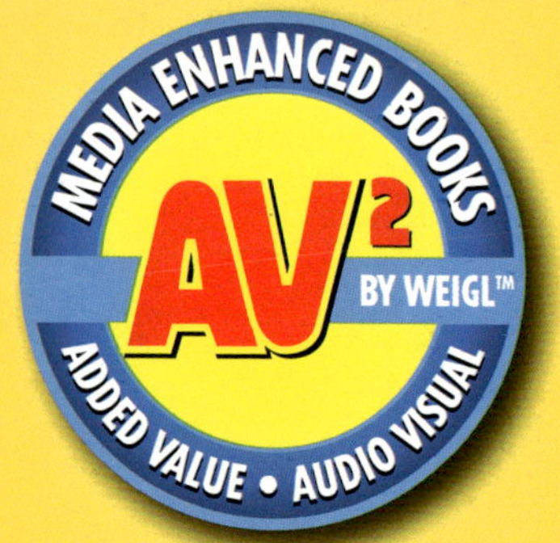

Go to www.av2books.com, and enter this book's unique code.

BOOK CODE

LBD49427

AV² by Weigl brings you media enhanced books that support active learning.

AV² provides enriched content that supplements and complements this book. Weigl's AV² books strive to create inspired learning and engage young minds in a total learning experience.

Your AV² Media Enhanced books come alive with...

Audio
Listen to sections of the book read aloud.

Key Words
Study vocabulary, and complete a matching word activity.

Video
Watch informative video clips.

Quizzes
Test your knowledge.

Embedded Weblinks
Gain additional information for research.

Slide Show
View images and captions, and prepare a presentation.

Try This!
Complete activities and hands-on experiments.

... and much, much more!

Published by AV² by Weigl
350 5th Avenue, 59th Floor
New York, NY 10118
Website: www.av2books.com

Library of Congress Control Number: 2017960028

ISBN 978-1-4896-7364-0 (hardcover)
ISBN 978-1-4896-7958-1 (softcover)
ISBN 978-1-4896-7365-7 (multi-user eBook)

Printed in the United States of America in Brainerd, Minnesota
1 2 3 4 5 6 7 8 9 0 22 21 20 19 18

012018
120817

Project Coordinator: John Willis Art Director: Terry Paulhus

Every reasonable effort has been made to trace ownership and to obtain permission to reprint copyright material. The publisher would be pleased to have any errors or omissions brought to its attention so that they may be corrected in subsequent printings.

Weigl acknowledges Getty Images, Newscom, and Alamy as its primary image suppliers for this title.

French Bulldogs

Contents

Name That Dog

What dog has a flat face and ears like a bat?

What dog snorts and snuffles?

What dog is sometimes called the "frog dog"?

What dog is popular with many movie stars?

Did you say the French bulldog?

You are right!

Monsieur Bulldog

French bulldogs are thought to be descended from a British breed. These small dogs were favorites among British **lace** makers in the 1850s. Eventually, their owners moved to France, and these dogs were bred with other types of dogs, such as pugs and terriers. They became popular with both **rural** landowners and **fashionable** ladies in the city. It was not long before this small dog became known as the *boules-dogue francais*, or "French bulldog."

Great Britain and France are separated by a body of water called the English Channel. The shortest distance between the two countries is 21 miles (34 kilometers).
Ireland
England
Wales
Great Britain
English Channel
Denmark
Belgium
Germany
Bay of Biscay
France
Switzerland
Italy
Spain
Mediterranean Sea

In 1898, the French Bulldog Club of America had its first show in the Waldorf Astoria ballroom, in New York City. In 1912, the breed was officially named the French bulldog by the English Kennel Club. In 1913, the Westminster Kennel Club show had 100 French bulldog entries. The French bulldog was starting to become a popular breed of dog.

Over the years, interest in the French bulldog decreased. However, beginning in the early 2000s, the breed became very popular again. Today, many people refer to them by the nickname "Frenchies."

The French bulldog was bred to be a **companion**. Its small stature makes it a good indoor dog. It also helps out as a **watchdog**, alerting its owners to visitors.

According to the American Kennel Club (AKC), the French bulldog is ranked as the sixth-favorite breed in the United States today.

Most French bulldogs can be adopted for a few hundred dollars. Frenchies with rare coloring, such as blue, can cost up to $30,000.

The Beautiful French Bulldog

The French bulldog is small and **stocky**. Its short legs, wide chest, and pear-shaped body give it a sturdy look. Although they have a flattened face and an **underbite**, which gives them a grumpy appearance, these dogs are very lovable.

French bulldogs stand 11 to 13 inches (28 to 33 centimeters) tall at the shoulders. A healthy weight is between 16 and 28 pounds (7 and 13 kilograms). French bulldogs can sometimes eat too much, so their food must be carefully monitored.

Flat-faced breeds like French bulldogs are known as *brachycephalic*. The word comes from Greek words meaning "short" and "head."

French bulldogs have large eyes. Their eyes can give them a lot of personality. However, they can be scratched very easily. It is important to be careful around a French bulldog's face.

They also have bat-like ears that stand straight up. These dogs always look very alert. Their tails can be straight or curled in a corkscrew shape.

French bulldogs have short, fine hair. They do not shed very much. Their fur can be black, red, white, **fawn**, or **brindle**. Their coat is silky and soft, and their skin is loose, which makes them appealing to pet.

In Great Britain, French bulldogs are often called “pigdogs” because of their unique looks and goofy personalities.

A Good Temperament

French bulldogs are very friendly, approachable dogs. They love to **socialize** with children and adults. They can be friendly with other animals, but prefer dogs to cats.

French bulldogs are known to be **mischievous**. They crave attention and will often be the "clown." Once trained, they are well behaved. They are quiet dogs, barking only to let their owner know someone has arrived.

French bulldogs have plenty of energy for games. This makes them great playmates for children.

French bulldogs do well in cities. According to the AKC, in 2017 they were the most popular breed of dog in New York City.

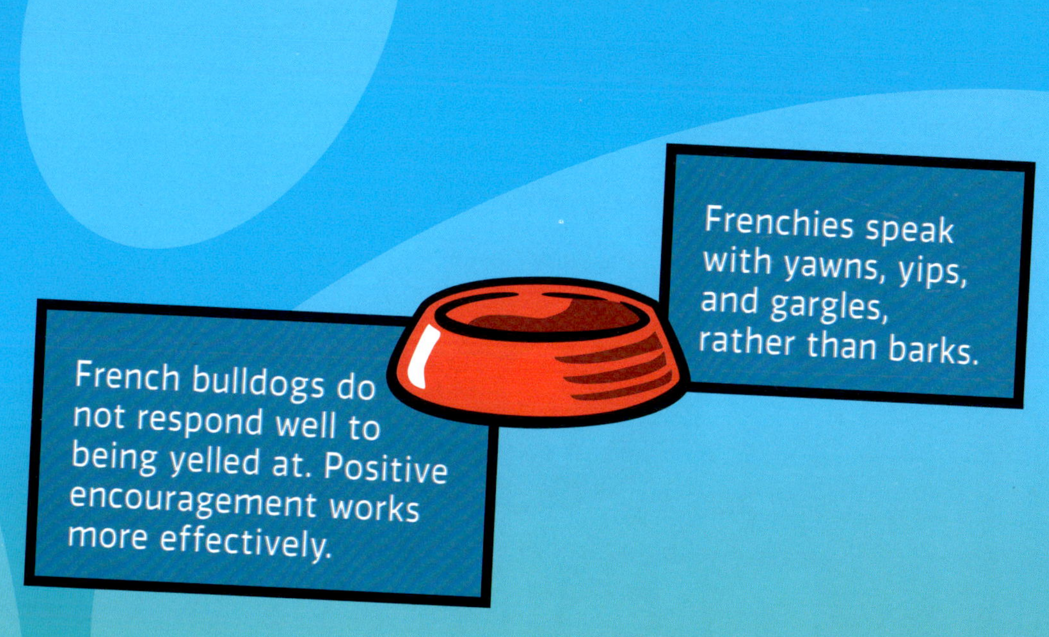

French bulldogs take a lot of work to train because they can be stubborn. It is best to start training them as puppies in short sessions. Treats can be a good **incentive**. It can take up to six months to house-train a French bulldog. However, once it is trained, it will remember what it has learned.

French bulldogs require a short walk every day. They do not need a lot of activity. They are excellent indoor dogs and become good, quiet companions. Older people may enjoy French bulldogs as pets. They are very happy to curl up on a lap or sit next to their owners for a snuggle.

Playful Puppies

French bulldog mothers have three or four puppies in a litter. Sometimes, litters may have five puppies, but that is unusual.

A one-week-old French bulldog puppy weighs about 2 pounds (1 kg). The puppy doubles its weight by the time it is around two weeks old. Like all puppies, French bulldogs enjoy play. It is important to spend time with French bulldog puppies so that they can get used to people.

For the first few weeks, French bulldog puppies are only awake for two or three hours a day.

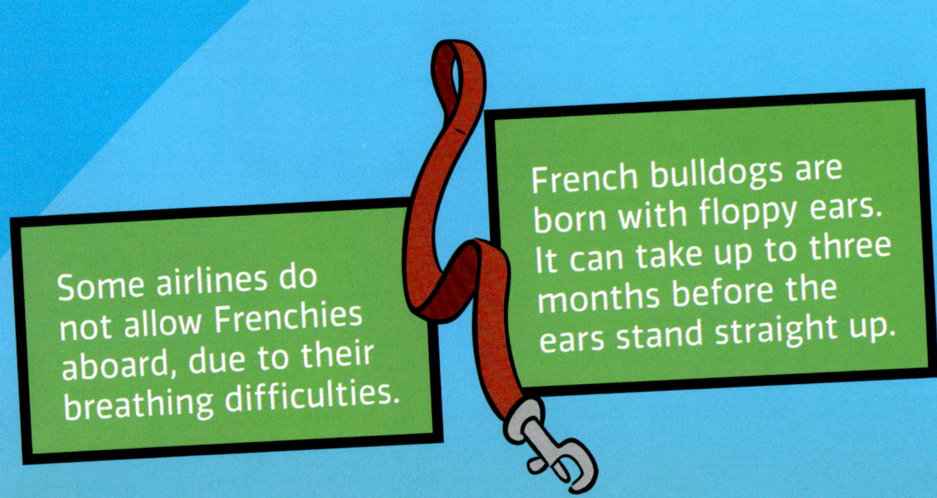

Unlike many dogs, French bulldogs cannot swim. It is important to watch puppies around water so they do not accidentally fall in. Even as adult dogs, French bulldogs should wear life vests if they are going to be near water.

French bulldog puppies require a lot of attention and training. They need a space that is their own. A puppy sweater or vest is a good idea for short winter walks. They enjoy having some toys to play with as well.

French bulldogs of all ages should get at least 30 minutes of exercise a day, even in cold weather.

French bulldogs are very social, but they are also quiet dogs. This helps make them good companions for older adults.

A Friendly Companion

French bulldogs are too friendly to make good guard dogs. They can serve as watchdogs, but are also gentle, welcoming hosts. Their temperament makes them excellent companions for people of all ages. With training, they can be good **therapy** dogs. Therapy dogs are meant to give emotional support and company to people who need it. For someone who needs a special friend, a French bulldog is a good choice.

"Frenchies" in Film

French bulldogs have often been featured in films. They are good actors. In the movie *Titanic*, a French bulldog is seen boarding the ship and walking the deck. His "character" is based on the real documentation of a French bulldog named Gamin de Pycombe. This Frenchie accompanied his owner, Robert Williams Daniel, aboard the *Titanic*. Leonardo DiCaprio, the star of *Titanic*, has a Frenchie himself.

In the film *Secondhand Lions*, a young boy is left on a farm to live with his uncles and an assortment of animals, including an old lion. A chunky, white French bulldog greets the boy in the beginning and becomes one of his friends as he gets used to his new home.

French bulldogs are often called "frog dogs" because of the way they stretch out their hind legs when they lie down.

Linus the French Bulldog has been featured in multiple films, including *Just Married*, *Bringing Down the House*, and *Secondhand Lions*.

French bulldogs should be bathed about once a month.

Grooming French Bulldogs

French bulldogs should be brushed weekly to keep their coats shiny and soft. Their short hair never needs to be trimmed. They do need to have their nails clipped once a month, because their nails do not wear down naturally. It is best for a professional groomer to do this task.

A French bulldog needs its teeth brushed regularly to keep them clean and to have fresh breath. Cleaning a French bulldog's ears with a damp cloth and rubbing them with some natural oil is a good idea. The oil will help their skin to stay hydrated.

French bulldogs cannot **regulate** their body temperature, so extreme heat or cold is not safe for them. If they get overheated, they may get heat stroke. In places where it is cold in the winter or hot in the summer, French bulldogs must live indoors. In extreme weather, these dogs cannot be left outside for very long.

All dogs should have regular visits to a **veterinarian**. French bulldogs need checkups to ensure they are in good health. Like many **thoroughbred** dogs, Frenchies can have health issues. They might have breathing problems. They may also experience spinal disorders or have eye or joint issues. With care, these dogs can live for 11 to 13 years.

Adult French bulldogs should visit the vet once or twice a year. Most enjoy the extra attention.

French Bulldog Quiz

Q: Which American city held the first official French bulldog show?

A: New York City

Q: Who were the original owners of the earliest French bulldogs?

A: English lace makers

Q: How much does the average French bulldog weigh?

A: 16–28 pounds (7–13 kg)

Q: What can happen if a Frenchie becomes overheated?

A: It can get heat stroke.

Q: Can French bulldogs swim?

A: No

Q: What is the differenc between French bulldog puppy ears and adult ea

ppies are born with floppy ears,
h straighten up over a few weeks
onths.

Key Words

brindle (BRIN-duhl): a brownish color with streaks of other color

companion (kum-PAN-yuhn): a person or animal with whom one spends a lot of time

fashionable (FASH-uh-nub-ul): representing a current popular trend

fawn (FAHN): a light yellowish-brown color

incentive (in-SEN-tiv): a thing that encourages a person or animal to do something

lace (LACE): fine, open fabric of cotton or linen

mischievous (MISS-chih-vuss): causing trouble in a playful way

regulate (REG-yuh-late): to control

rural (RUR-ul): countryside

socialize (SOH-shuh-lize): to mix with others

stocky (STOK-ee): thick, sturdy

therapy (THER-uh-pee): treatment, help

thoroughbred (THUR-oh-bred): of pure breed

underbite (UN-dur-bite): the projection of the lower teeth beyond the upper

veterinarian (vet-rih-NAIR-ee-un): an animal doctor

watchdog (WACH-dog): a dog kept to guard a private property

Index

Log on to www.av2books.com

AV² by Weigl brings you media enhanced books that support active learning. Go to www.av2books.com, and enter the special code found on page 2 of this book. You will gain access to enriched and enhanced content that supplements and complements this book. Content includes video, audio, weblinks, quizzes, a slide show, and activities.

AV² Online Navigation

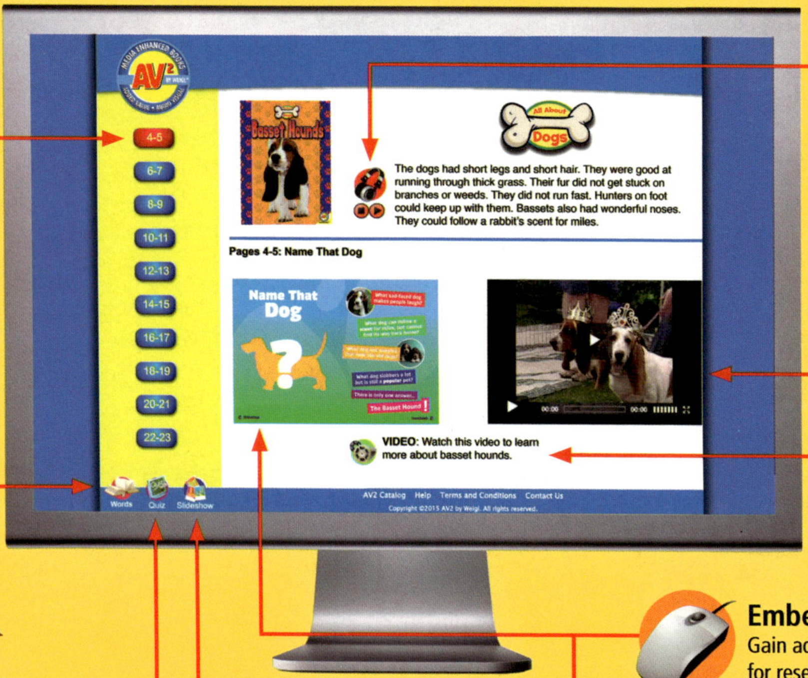

Audio
Listen to sections of the book read aloud.

Book Pages
AV² pages directly correspond to pages in the book.

Video
Watch informative video clips.

Embedded Weblinks
Gain additional information for research.

Key Words
Study vocabulary, and complete a matching word activity.

Try This!
Complete activities and hands-on experiments.

Quizzes
Test your knowledge.

Slide Show
View images and captions, and prepare a presentation.

AV² was built to bridge the gap between print and digital. We encourage you to tell us what you like and what you want to see in the future.

Sign up to be an AV² Ambassador at www.av2books.com/ambassador.

Due to the dynamic nature of the Internet, some of the URLs and activities provided as part of AV² by Weigl may have changed or ceased to exist. AV² by Weigl accepts no responsibility for any such changes. All media enhanced books are regularly monitored to update addresses and sites in a timely manner. Contact AV² by Weigl at 1-866-649-3445 or av2books@weigl.com with any questions, comments, or feedback.